Cornerstones of Freedom

The Story of

CLARA BARTON

By Zachary Kent

Illustrated by Ralph Canaday

WITHDRAWN

⏂ CHILDRENS PRESS ®

CHICAGO

Library of Congress Cataloging-in-Publication Data

Kent, Zachary.
　The story of Clara Barton.

　(Cornerstones of freedom)
　Summary: Presents the life and career of the nurse
who, after fearlessly serving on the battlefields of the
Civil War, founded the American Red Cross.
　　1.　Barton, Clara, 1821-1912—Juvenile literature.
2.　Red Cross—Biography—Juvenile literature.
3.　American National Red Cross—Juvenile literature.
4.　Nurses—United States—Biography—Juvenile literature.
[1.　Barton, Clara, 1821-1912. 2. Nurses] I. Canaday,
Ralph, ill. II. Title. III. Series.
HV569.B3K45 1987　　 361.7′634′0924 [B] [92]　86-29899
ISBN 0-516-04725-6

Hundreds of wounded soldiers lay upon the ground, moaning and screaming in pain. Some cried out for help, while others begged for a little food or a taste of water. In crude hospital tents, surgeons worked feverishly to save as many lives as possible. They amputated mangled arms and legs, cut out bullets and shell fragments, and bandaged bloody chest and head wounds.

The Battle of Cedar Mountain was over. The Confederate and Union armies that had clashed here on August 9, 1862, had moved on. But four days later the horrible aftermath of their fight remained, littering the Virginia battlefield. Now, as the thunder of distant cannon cracked the night, one small woman in a plain black skirt and jacket moved among the injured. With love and devotion Clara Barton helped these soldiers, Northern and

Southern alike, in any way she could. After receiving a cracker or a comforting word from her, hardened troopers wept with gratitude for this woman who seemed to have dropped from heaven.

Army doctor James I. Dunn reported: "She appeared in front of the hospital at twelve o'clock at night with a four-mule team loaded with everything needed; and at a time when we were entirely out of dressings of every kind, she supplied us with everything, and while the shells were bursting in every direction . . . she staid [sic] dealing out shirts to the naked wounded, and preparing soup and seeing it prepared in all the hospitals. . . . I thought that night if heaven ever sent out a homely angel, she must be one, her assistance was so timely."

In an age when American women were expected to stay at home, Clara Barton refused to remain idle while brave soldiers bled. "When our armies fought on Cedar Mountain," she later wrote, "I broke the shackles and went to the field." Her labors that August night marked the start of her professional nursing career. Before long, people throughout the North spoke of Clara Barton as the "Angel of the Battlefield." When the Civil War ended in 1865 her service to the nation did not stop, for she went on to found the American Red Cross in 1882.

The youngest in her family, Clara Barton was born on December 25, 1821. Though she had few playmates her own age, growing up in the Bartons' modest home in North Oxford, Massachusetts, provided her with a childhood full of fun and learning activity. Her brother David taught her horseback riding, while other family members often read with her. Clara's father, Stephen Barton, was a veteran of the Ohio Indian wars. Later Clara recalled, "I listened breathlessly to his war stories."

At eleven years of age Clara performed her first nursing duties. A fall from a barn roof beam seriously injured David Barton. For the next two years Clara stayed by her brother's bedside, watching over him night and day. Only after he regained his health did she return to school.

An intelligent, ambitious, though timid young woman, at seventeen Clara chose to become a teacher. In 1839 she began teaching classes in Oxford's one-room schoolhouses. During the next ten years her success as a teacher grew. Eventually the school board asked her to teach in the roughest district schools. Fully aware of her skills, Clara demanded pay equal to a man's. "I may sometimes be willing to teach for nothing," she told her employers, "but if paid at all, I shall never do a man's work for less than a man's pay."

More than one neighborhood man fell in love with Clara's spirit of independence. Instead of marrying, however, Clara decided in 1850 to quit teaching for a while and "find a school . . . to teach *me* something." For a year she enrolled in the Clinton Liberal Institute in Clinton, New York.

When her studies ended she visited friends in Bordentown, New Jersey, and welcomed an opportunity

to take up teaching in Bordentown's private
subscription school. She enjoyed instructing the
pupils there, but while walking about town she
noticed many boys standing idle. "Lady, there is no
school for us," explained one fourteen-year-old. "We
would be glad to go if there was one." Immediately
Clara Barton determined to establish a public school
that *all* children could attend, regardless of their
ability to pay. With six hundred students, Bordentown's first free school soon proved so popular that
the town built a new schoolhouse. Though Clara
clearly deserved the position, a man was hired as
principal. "I could bear the ingratitude," insisted

Clara, "but not the pettiness and jealousy of this
principal." Terribly upset, she resigned her teaching
job in early 1854 and left for Washington, D.C.,
where she hoped to "do something decided."

In Washington Clara found work as a clerk in the
U.S. Patent Office. No other woman was employed
by the Federal government at that time. Required
to copy important documents, after just three
months Clara revealed: "I have filled a *great* volume
almost as heavy as I can lift. My arm is tired, and
my poor thumb is all calloused holding my pen."
Before long, her honesty and competence made her
invaluable to the Commissioner of Patents.

During visits to the Capitol, Clara heard raging arguments in Congress over the issue of slavery. In March of 1861 she witnessed the inauguration of Abraham Lincoln as president and sensed that the nation would soon be torn in two by civil war. "This conflict is one thing I've been waiting for," she exclaimed. "I'm well and strong and young—young enough to go to the front. If I can't be a soldier, I'll help soldiers."

In April the Civil War began when Southern militiamen attacked Fort Sumter in Charleston harbor. Soon after, the Sixth Massachusetts Regiment arrived to help defend Washington. Clara rushed to greet these soldiers, many of them old friends and former pupils. At their temporary quarters in the Capitol's Senate chamber, Clara found that "her boys" lacked personal supplies. Quickly she returned home "to tear up old sheets for towels and handkerchiefs." She filled a large market basket with "serving utensils, thread, needles, thimbles, scissors, pins, buttons," and other items and handed them out to the needy. In the following months she wrote to the soldiers' families, collecting preserved fruits, blankets, candles, and other supplies, until her apartment looked like a warehouse. All these

things she distributed to the Union troops before they set off for Virginia.

As the war continued into 1862, Clara realized that after every bloody fight the wounded soldiers were left to suffer. Many died of thirst and neglect before they could be brought to Washington's hospitals. Nurses were urgently needed on the battlefields, and forty-year-old Clara determined to go. Her struggle to receive permission from the army was finally rewarded in August 1862. Clutching her written passes, she climbed onto a wagon loaded with nursing supplies and headed into Virginia. At Cedar Mountain she proved her worth, feeding soldiers and making bandages. As more battles followed, she returned again and again to the field.

After the Second Battle of Bull Run on August 31, Clara rushed by train to Fairfax Station to help the arriving wounded. "The men," she explained, "were brought down from the field and laid on the ground beside the train and so back up the hill till they covered acres. . . . By midnight there must have been three thousand helpless men." Using every "can, jar, bucket, bowl, cup or tumbler" she found among the station's supplies, Clara handed out food, soup, and coffee to these soldiers, taking care not to step on them in the dark. Near the Chantilly battlefield a few days later she fed the wounded a gruel she mixed of crushed crackers, wine, whiskey, water, and brown sugar. For five rainy days she worked, taking only a two-hour nap in all that time.

Then Clara learned that a major battle was to take place in Maryland. Wasting no time, she joined the Union army's long wagon train with her own heavy wagon. "Follow the cannon," Clara insisted, and through the night her tired driver pressed forward. They ended up beside Antietam Creek on September 17, 1862, the bloodiest single day of the Civil War. While giving one wounded man a drink of water, a bullet first tore through her sleeve and then struck the soldier, killing him. Later another soldier with a bullet in his jaw begged Clara to cut it out. "Opening the best blade of my pocket-knife," she recounted, "I extracted the ball and washed and bandaged the face."

Regardless of danger, Clara remained fearless. At the Battle of Fredericksburg, in December 1862, she nursed injured soldiers brought to the Lacy House. "A shell shattered the door of the room in which she was attending to wounded men," remembered another volunteer. "She did not flinch but continued her duties as usual." Soon a message arrived from a surgeon working across the river in the town of Fredericksburg itself. Clara opened the bloody slip of paper and read the doctor's hurried request: "Come to me. Your place is here."

Without a thought for her safety, she crossed a swaying pontoon bridge while bullets whistled all around her. At the end of the bridge a gallant officer stepped up to help her. "While our hands were raised," Clara later wrote, "a piece of an exploding shell hissed through between us, just below our arms, carrying away a portion . . . of his coat and my dress." She hastened forward to the hospital, but in another half hour she saw this kind officer again, when he was brought in dead.

All that afternoon she tended the wounded in Fredericksburg. While wiping the blood from one soldier's face, she discovered the man was the sexton from her old home church. Later she returned to the Lacy House, where she found twelve hundred bleeding troopers jammed into the twelve rooms. The house was so crowded that wounded men lay under tables and on cupboard shelves. "Ease pain, soothe sorrow, lessen suffering"—these were Clara's only thoughts as she nursed these men.

Though she might have joined the five hundred nurses of the United States Sanitary Commission, Clara Barton preferred to remain her own boss. In April 1863 she sailed to Hilton Head Island off the coast of South Carolina. For eight months the Union army and navy in that coastal region had been attacking the city of Charleston. During her time there, Clara nursed soldiers feverish with malaria and bandaged others wounded on the battlefields of Morris Island and Fort Wagner.

Back in Washington, Clara's services were suddenly called for in May 1864 when, as she later wrote, "the terrible slaughter of the Wilderness and Spotsylvania turned all pitying hearts . . . once more to Fredericksburg." Rushing to the Belle Plain boat landing, Clara found two hundred loaded ambulance wagons waiting for river transportation north. A recent rain had turned the plain into a sea of mud. "No hub of a wheel was in sight," she exclaimed, "and you saw nothing of any animal below its knees." Pinning up her apron and filling it with crackers, Clara waded from wagon to wagon to feed the starving wounded.

Following the horrors of the Wilderness campaign, General Benjamin Butler invited Clara to serve as supervisor of nurses for the Union army. Of a typical day at one hospital she informed a friend, "I have cooked ten dozen eggs . . . washed hands and face, put ice on hot heads, mustard on cold feet, written six soldiers' letters home, stood beside three death beds . . . and now at this hour, midnight, I am too sleepy and stupid to write." Devotedly, Clara stayed here throughout the war's final battles.

After Robert E. Lee's surrender at Appomattox Court House ended the war in April 1865, Clara Barton quickly found another way to use her talents. With President Lincoln's official approval, she established an agency to find and identify many of the thousands of men missing as a result of the war. In the next months Clara received bushels of letters from families whose loved ones had not returned home from the army. In newspapers throughout the country she published lists of the missing. Noticing familiar names, ex-soldiers wrote to her confirming the fates of comrades lost in the fighting. During four years' work, the inquiries of Barton's "Office of Correspondence" brought information to more than 22,000 American families.

Clara's greatest achievement during this time occurred in July 1865, when she traveled to the site of the Andersonville prison camp in Sumter County, Georgia. Buried in the sandy soil here lay more than thirteen thousand Union soldiers who had died in prison. With a crew of laborers and the help of young Dorence Atwater, a former prisoner who had kept careful records, Clara provided identifying markers for all but 440 of the graves. Today the camp at Andersonville is a national cemetery.

Throughout the war Clara spent every penny of her income buying nursing supplies. With the country at peace at last, she decided to earn a living as a lecturer. Beginning in October 1866, she toured hundreds of Northern towns and cities giving her talk on "Work and Incidents of the War." People eager to see the famous "Angel of the Battlefield" jammed halls and auditoriums when she came to speak. They marveled to think that the five-foot, three-inch woman standing shyly on the lecture platform could have accomplished so much. Her stories of soldiers' suffering and bravery moved her audiences to tears, applause, and cheering. Finally, however, the strain of her heavy speaking schedule proved to be too great. In the winter of 1868 Clara suffered a sudden breakdown, losing her voice for a time. Under doctor's orders, she set sail for Europe to take a long-deserved rest.

Through 1869 Clara Barton traveled in England, France, and Corsica. It was during a stay in Geneva, Switzerland, that she first learned of the Red Cross. After witnessing the agonies of the Battle of Solferino in 1864, a Genevan named Jean-Henri Dunant wrote a book describing his experiences. At the end of *A Memory of Solferino* Dunant wondered,

"Would it not be possible, in time of peace, to form relief societies for the purpose of having care given to the wounded in wartime?" Inspired by these words, twelve nations at the Geneva Convention of 1864 signed a treaty forming the International Red Cross. Its purpose was to help wounded and sick soldiers, prisoners of war, and civilians under wartime conditions.

When war broke out between France and Prussia in the summer of 1870, Clara observed firsthand the work of the Red Cross. Eager to help wherever she could, she forgot her own illness and hurried toward the sound of battle. Time after time she came upon Red Cross volunteers and greatly admired their efforts. "No mistakes, no needless suffering," she recalled. "No starving, no lack of care . . . but order, plenty, cleanliness, and comfort wherever that little flag made its way . . . I said to myself, 'If I live to return to my country, I will try to make my people understand the Red Cross and that treaty.'"

As the fighting raged on, Clara used her skills and influence to establish hospitals and raise money for refugees. From the city of Strasbourg she wrote in May 1871: "Thousands who are well today will rot with smallpox and be devoured by body-lice before the end of August. Against . . . these two scourges there is, I believe, no check but the destruction of all infected garments." Immediately she founded a sewing center which provided clean clothing for the needy poor. For her work here and in other cities during the Franco-Prussian War, Clara Barton received the official thanks of European noblemen and governments.

Completely exhausted, Clara returned to the United States in 1873 and settled in the restful town of Danville, New York. As her health improved she remembered her desire to establish the Red Cross in America. During the next seven years she struggled to promote the organization. She published a pamphlet entitled, "What The Red Cross Is" to inform the American public. It included her original idea that the Red Cross should provide aid during peacetime disasters also. She wrote to senators and statesmen urging the adoption of the Geneva treaty. At meetings with Presidents Rutherford B. Hayes, James A. Garfield, and Chester A. Arthur she fervently pressed her cause. Finally on March 16, 1882, the Senate ratified the Geneva Convention, and at the age of sixty, Clara Barton became first president of the American Red Cross.

Even before the news became final, local Red
Cross societies were meeting in Danville, Syracuse,
and Rochester, New York. When fires swept
through the forests of Michigan in the fall of 1881
these Red Cross chapters raised eighty thousand
dollars. With the help of Julian Hubbell, her chief
field agent, Clara distributed this money to
Michigan's fire victims.

In 1882 the Mississippi River overflowed, pouring over millions of acres of cotton and sugar lands. "The swift rising floods," exclaimed Clara, "overtook . . . man and beast in their flight of terror . . . leaving them clinging in . . . despair to some trembling roof or swaying tree-top till relief could reach and rescue them." After Clara made a national appeal for help, Red Cross workers hastened to the region with medicine, clothing, bedding, and shelter. Stricken farmers even received supplies of tools, seeds, and lumber to aid them in rebuilding their lives.

In 1884, both the Mississippi and the Ohio rivers flooded. Helpless families along the swollen riverbanks waved and cheered when they saw the approaching smoke of the Red Cross steamships *Josh V. Throop* and *Mattie Belle.* From Cincinnati to New Orleans these boats carried vital help to flood victims.

Under Clara Barton's guidance and personal direction, the Red Cross continued its good work all through the 1880s. Whether the disaster was an earthquake in Charleston, South Carolina, or a tornado in Mount Vernon, Illinois, Clara Barton and her workers were always early on the scene.

One of the most serious disasters the American
Red Cross responded to in its early days was the
Johnstown flood of May 1889. After heavy rains, a
dam broke on the Conemaugh River nine miles
above Johnstown, Pennsylvania. A violent, thirty-
foot wall of water suddenly crashed down through
the city, killing more than two thousand people,
sweeping houses away, and destroying millions of
dollars worth of property. In five days' time, Clara
Barton arrived on the first train that got through.
Setting up her headquarters in a tent and using a

dry-goods box for a desk, she directed an army of fifty Red Cross workers. Over the next five months the Red Cross handed out half a million dollars worth of aid. Red Cross carpenters even hammered together temporary three-story hotels to house the homeless. When their work was done at last, the Johnstown *Daily Tribune* wrote: "How shall we thank Miss Clara Barton and the Red Cross for the help they have given us? It cannot be done. . . . We cannot thank Miss Barton in words. . . . Try to describe the sunshine. . . . Words fail."

Again in 1892, when news reached the United States of crop failure and famine in Russia, the American Red Cross responded. Generous Americans gave money, and Iowans even contributed 225 train cars of corn for the Red Cross to distribute in Russia. In 1896 Clara Barton also traveled abroad to offer relief assistance to Armenian massacre victims during the religious wars in Turkey. These early activities nobly pioneered the idea of peacetime foreign aid.

During Cuba's war of independence from Spain in 1898, Clara was already in Cuba helping suffering civilians when the USS *Maine* mysteriously exploded in Havana harbor. Angry Americans blamed the sinking on the Spanish. When the United States declared war on that country in April, the American Red Cross began its first official wartime service. Army doctors welcomed Red Cross nurses at Cuban field hospitals, where men suffering from ugly wounds and tropical diseases needed care. Red Cross relief supplies arrived by the ton, and Clara personally oversaw their distribution.

Clara was greatly honored for her many services in Cuba. Upon the surrender of the city of Santiago, the U.S. Navy allowed the Red Cross relief ship

State of Texas into the harbor before any other vessel. As the boat proudly steamed forward, Clara stood on the deck and led Red Cross workers in the singing of "America."

Though no one could doubt Clara's dedication as Red Cross president, as she grew older people worried about her continued ability. A coworker wrote, "The National Red Cross Association in this country has been Miss Clara Barton, and Miss Clara Barton has been the National Red Cross Society." But many Red Cross members believed it was time for Clara to step down. Under pressure, in May 1904, eighty-three-year-old Clara Barton resigned her position as president.

Clara retired to her home in Glen Echo, Maryland. The former National Red Cross Headquarters, this great barnlike structure was built with lumber used during the Johnstown flood. Here Clara entertained guests, answered letters, and began her autobiography, *The Story of My Childhood.* Rising early every day, she milked cows, fed chickens, and tended her vegetable garden.

After a lifetime among death and danger, Clara Barton died at last on April 12, 1912, at the age of ninety. All the nation mourned her death. A New York City wagon driver, seeing her coffin on the way to its burial place in Massachusetts, exclaimed: "Is it possible? Why, my father was a Confederate soldier and at the Battle of Antietam he was wounded in the neck and was bleeding to death, when Miss Barton found him . . . and bound up his wounds in time to save his life."

The "Angel of the Battlefield" had saved many such lives during her long years of caring public service. Through her work with the Red Cross she brought hope to many millions more. Even today, after world wars and scores of natural disasters, the good work of the American Red Cross continues, a living memorial to its founder, Clara Barton.

About the Author

Zachary Kent grew up in the town of Little Falls, New Jersey. He is a graduate of St. Lawrence University and holds a teaching certificate in English. Following college he was employed at a New York City literary agency for two years until he decided to launch a career as a writer. To support himself while writing, he has worked as a taxi driver, a shipping clerk, and a house painter.

Mr. Kent has had a lifelong interest in American history. As a boy the study of the United States presidents was his special hobby. His collection of presidential items includes books, pictures, and games, as well as several autographed letters.

About the Artist

Ralph Canaday has been involved in all aspects of commercial art since graduation from the Art Institute of Chicago in 1959. He is an illustrator, designer, painter, and sculptor whose work has appeared in many national publications, textbooks, and corporate promotional materials. Mr. Canaday lives in Hanover Park, Illinois, with his wife Arlene, who is also in publishing.